By Rays
of
Light

By Rays of Light

Carroll Blair

Aveon Publishing Company

ISBN: 978-1-936430-35-2

Library of Congress Control Number
2011902863

Aveon Publishing Co.
P.O. Box 380739
Cambridge, MA 02238-0739 USA

Also by Carroll Blair

1

What is life for but to

embrace its miracle, to taste

of its magnificence with

all the senses . . .

2

What day is not a gift

of the sacred

3

Nothing is more magical

than life itself

4

Wonder opens all doors

to truth, to love, to joy

5

The lessons of life have a

beginning and an end,

but life's lesson has no

beginning and no end

6

Every day there is something new

to discover that has always been,

and something new to create

that has never been

7

To look upon everything as if

perceiving it for the first time . . .

the key to creative being

8

How much the light of the sun

shines upon delivering it from

darkness, and so much more

the light of the spirit

9

The open mind of wisdom —

the open heart of innocence —

the open soul of love . . .

like an open vessel forever

receiving without prejudice,

forever giving

without desire for reward

10

There are no honors to be gained

from the spiritual quest, just

treasure beyond imagining

11

Everything comes on the wings

of Possibility

12

One must wake to the dream

before one may dream

to the awakening

13

Lives, as temporal streams

flowing into eternal rivers,

flowing into eternal sea

14

Every moment the world

comes into being in the

appearance of the unchanging

15

Even of the visible

all has not been seen

16

Reality is not the sky, the mountain,

the valley, the river, the ocean . . .

it is that which manifests the

sky, the mountain, the valley,

the river, the ocean

17

It is in the space of life,

i.e., in the silence, where the

fullness of life's power is

most keenly sensed

18

When pregnant with the

highest gifts the spirit

draws its deepest silence

19

Before the first human to have

a thought or uttered a word

there was divine wisdom

waiting to speak

20

A second, a minute, a day,

a year . . . all one and the same

in the realm of the infinite

21

The eternal is a place

without time, where there

is no "place" to get to

22

How deeply immersed one must

be in the *now* to profoundly

appreciate the eternal

23

The spirit is not a house,

a city, a nation, a globe,

but a universe, with all

the power of the universe

24

The spirit is infinite in its

giving, but depth after depth

must be created for the giving

to be received

25

Where ego is present love
cannot enter; where ego is
present wisdom cannot
enter; where ego is present
peace cannot enter

26

Every seed needs its proper

soil to grow, including those

of the spiritual

27

The greatest nourishment neither

hands nor lips can touch

28

You want enlightenment but

don't know where to begin . . .

be still   do nothing —

seek not — want not —

there is your beginning . . .

(and more than your beginning)

29

There are examples around you

ever old, ever new of what is

false, of what is true

30

The power of what is great

never loses its strength;

the weakness of what is

trivial never fades

31

The profoundest illuminations of

life are those that transcend the

personal; that reach through

the soul of objectivity

into the universal

32

Love is more than an

emotion . . . it is a

state of heart

33

To never lose the ego

is to remain forever lost

34

Ego is a blind monster

that believes that it can see

35

The light opens to one

as much as one opens

to the light

36

One finds one's way to the

eternal through the labyrinth

of the temporal

37

Things seem to appear

out of nowhere to assist

those who are going

somewhere . . .

38

Like paper waiting to be

written on, like books

waiting to be read, the

spiritual journey

waiting to begin

39

True is the magic of the divine

40

To remove the banality from

your life is to make way

for the profound to enter

41

One either turns in the

direction of enlightenment

or away from it

42

How much love can I bring

to the world? How much light

can I project into the

darkness? . . . should not

these questions be asked

every day of one's life . . .

43

As the heart softens it strengthens

44

All good things grow

the more they are utilized

or given

45

Conscious effort becomes

subconscious grace

46

Discipline is the way to greater

enlightenment, and enlightenment

to greater discipline

47

One cannot search for knowledge

of any kind without learning

in the process something

about oneself

48

If one is sincere

in wanting to grow

one cannot fail

to grow

49

Life is an invitation to

experience; the opportunity

to explore, to see, to

aspire, to be

50

It is the temporal fire that

destroys, not the eternal

51

No one can teach to others

how to sing their life's song

52

Life's symphony, though

endless, can never be

fulfilled if you fail to

add your music to it

53

A world exists in every living

being, the nature of that world

different for each

54

To always do the best you

can with what you have

is to earn the state of

inner peace

55

It is the spiritual impulse that

gives birth to all that is noble

56

Each day of your life

a world is at stake . . .

your world

57

Inner depth is not

something that is

discovered, but something

that is created

58

When one is false, truths can

pass all around one, but cannot

help one; when one is true,

falsehood can attack from

all quarters, and one cannot

be harmed

59

The real voice of a

human being cannot be

heard by the ear, only

felt by the heart

60

The bounds of passion are

not as great as those of

compassion

61

A million candles can be lit

by the flame of a single

candle; a million souls

can be awakened by the

light of a single soul

62

Love is a force that haunts

with its beauty, with its nature,

ever present in the service

most valuable to the world

63

Like the center of existence,

like the home of the divine,

the center of love is nowhere

and everywhere

64

What is not to embrace

that is spoken without word . . .

65

Bliss too is of the sacred

66

More instructive, more important,

more precious than knowledge

is the profound sense of

wonder, for it is this that

leads to knowledge

(and so much more than

knowledge . . .)

67

What takes man out of himself

draws him closer to himself

68

There are arrivals on the

path of enlightenment,

but no Arrival

69

The highest place is that

of Placelessness

70

The universe too beckons

to be escaped from,

inviting man to go beyond

with the mind and spirit

that he's been given

71

Existence encompasses all,

the seen and the unseen,

from nothingness, to matter,

to all that is beyond matter

72

Life is equally

infinite in its microcosm

and macrocosm, and

as equally astonishing

73

There are miracles all

around you, and day and

night prayers abound

for a miracle

74

When one realizes that

there is something more,

how much of what

man has valued seems

so much less

75

The genesis of awakening

is quiet and still,

greeting its dawn

with a whispered kiss

76

There is light that cannot

be seen — only *sensed* . . .

77

The more the particulars

are pursued the less is

grasped of the whole

78

All is here when you

arrive; all is here when

you depart

79

To be one with that which

never dies is to know

the eternal in one's life

80

What is a spirit for but to

grow wings to soar to the

heights of what is grounded

in the sublime

81

To live in the state of

openness, receptive to the

unknown is to open oneself

to the measure of what can

be thought, can be felt,

can be known

82

How can a heart breathe,

a mind breathe, when

it is closed

83

Every moment is priceless —

how are they being spent . . .

are they being given to the

service of the priceless

84

Why is one born if not

to receive and bring forth

manifestation of the spiritual . . .

of the eternal

85

Life also has its fields of

pain, but they are where its

most beautiful flowers grow

86

If you want life to spare

you pain you want it to

spare you growth, insight,

depth, understanding, capacity

for the greatest love and joy

one can experience — you

want it to spare you   life

87

Are you interested in what

will bring you the least pain,

or bring you the most light

88

The spirit filled with love

has room for all things

89

To love is to love with

all one's life

90

When you surrender to love,

love surrenders to you

91

The greatest treasure cannot

be spent, only given

92

The world wants nothing

more from you than what

you have to give, but it

wants *all*

you have to give

93

Everyone is rich in their

moment of giving

94

The profound inhale and

exhale of a life . . . the

growing into oneself, and

the growing out of oneself

95

Silence . . . the realm of

the unutterable that

hails above all words

96

What is speechless may plant

seeds of inspiration that

one day sing to the world

97

The calm before the storm is

filled with serenity; the calm

after the storm, with ecstasy

98

To get to where there

is nothing left to say,

only everything to feel . . .

99

To live for the sake

of love . . . to love

for the sake of life . . .

100

Life itself is a prayer

unto itself

101

Nothing could exist if

not for an eternal force

present within

102

There is an end to all

you see before you, but

all does not come to an end

103

What remains has always been

104

To dream so that one may

discover reality . . . to seek

reality so that one may

dream more profoundly

105

Your mind, your heart,

your spirit is your

way home

106

Have faith in the journey

ABOUT THE AUTHOR

Carroll Blair is an author of more than twenty books and the recipient of numerous awards. His work has been well endorsed and commendably reviewed. Among his titles cited for distinction are *Through the Shadows*, winner of the Pacific Book Awards, and *Quarter Notes*, winner of the Sharp Writ Book Awards. He is an alumnus of the Boston Conservatory and lives in Massachusetts.